DATE DUE

APR. 13. 2000			

DEMCO 38-296

PABLO NERUDA
Nobel Prize-Winning Poet

David Goodnough

Enslow Publishers, Inc.

44 Fadem Road   PO Box 38
Box 699   Aldershot
Springfield, NJ 07081 Hants GU12 6BP
USA   UK

Library of Congress Cataloging-in-Publication Data

Goodnough, David.
    Pablo Neruda : Nobel prize-winning poet / David Goodnough.
        p. cm. — (Hispanic biographies)
    Summary: Traces the life and career, including the political activities,
of the famous Chilean poet.
    ISBN 0-7660-1042-2
    1. Neruda, Pablo, 1904–1973—Biography—Juvenile literature.
2. Poets, Chilean—20th century—Biography—Juvenile literature.
[1. Neruda, Pablo, 1904–1973. 2, Poets, Chilean.] I. Title. II. Series.
PQ8097.N4Z6483   1998
  861—dc21
  [B]
                                       97-32888
                                             CIP
                                           AC

Printed in the United States of America

10 9 8 7 6 5 4 3 2 1

Illustration Credits: Authorized by the Pablo Neruda Foundation, pp.
13, 17, 25, 28, 47, 83, 90, 97; Organization of American States, pp.
7, 31, 103, 113; Recreated by Enslow Publishers, Inc., pp. 9, 40, 54;
© Corel Corporation, pp. 57, 61; Maryknoll Fathers and Brothers, p.
73; AP/Wide World Photos, p. 100; Library of Congress, p. 111.

Cover Illustration: Authorized by the Pablo Neruda Foundation

CONTENTS

CHAPTER ONE

THE FUGITIVE

In 1948, Pablo Neruda was forty-three years old and on his way to becoming one of the world's best known and most beloved poets. At that time, however, he was also well known as a diplomat and politician in his native country of Chile, in South America. He had already served as his country's representative in Burma, Spain, and Mexico, and in 1945 he had been elected to his country's Senate. He had written and published poetry since he was a teenager and was now working on a long poem that was to make him even more famous. But, suddenly, he was running for his life.

On February 5, the Supreme Court of Chile had ordered Neruda's arrest. This came after he had been dismissed from the Senate for giving a fiery speech attacking the policies of the country's new president, Gabriel González Videla. As strange as it may seem, Neruda had been González Videla's national campaign manager during the recent election. He had become an enemy of González Videla after the new president had failed to fulfill his promises of reform, had imposed a strict censorship on the Chilean press, and had ordered the arrest of anyone who opposed him. Years later, Neruda was to say of González Videla that he had "turned into a vile, bloodthirsty vampire" and that this "contemptible creature had an insignificant but twisted mind."[1] These were strong words, but Neruda was never one to conceal his feelings.

Neruda went into hiding, and with the help of political allies and friends he was moved from house to house in cities throughout Chile. "I passed through fields, ports, cities, camps, and was in the homes of peasants, engineers, lawyers, seamen, doctors, miners," he later remembered.[2] After a year and a half of hiding out, Neruda agreed to be smuggled out of Chile across the Andes Mountains into neighboring Argentina. He left Santiago, Chile's capital city, in a car driven by a man he knew only as Escobar. Neruda wore a false beard and dark eyeglasses, and was covered with blankets in the rear seat of the car. On the

Gabriel González Videla, president of Chile from 1946 to 1952, ordered Pablo Neruda's arrest in 1948 for criticizing his regime.

way, they passed through his childhood home of Temuco, in southern Chile. "It was my childhood saying goodbye," he later wrote.[3]

After they left Temuco, their car was flagged down by a police officer standing in the middle of the road. Luckily, the man was just hitching a ride and asked them to give him a lift to a destination about sixty miles down the road. The officer sat up front with Escobar, while Neruda huddled in the backseat, pretending to be asleep. This was their only close call on the rest of the trip to their next hideout. This was a lumber camp in the foothills of the Andes run by Jorge Bellet, a man Neruda hardly knew. Bellet was to be in charge of the expedition across the mountains. Victor Bianchi, an old friend of Neruda's, would accompany Neruda and Escobar the rest of the way. The small party, joined by some expert horsemen and scouts, set off into the wilderness. "There were no tracks and no paths," Neruda recalled in 1971, "and I and my companions, riding on horseback, pressed forward on our tortuous way, avoiding the obstacles set by huge trees, impossible rivers, immense cliffs and desolate expanses of snow, blindly seeking the quarter in which my own liberty lay."[4] After traveling all day and most of the night, they reached an abandoned shack that marked the frontier between Chile and Argentina.

In Argentina, Neruda was not much safer than he had been in Chile. He was a fugitive, and the

Chile

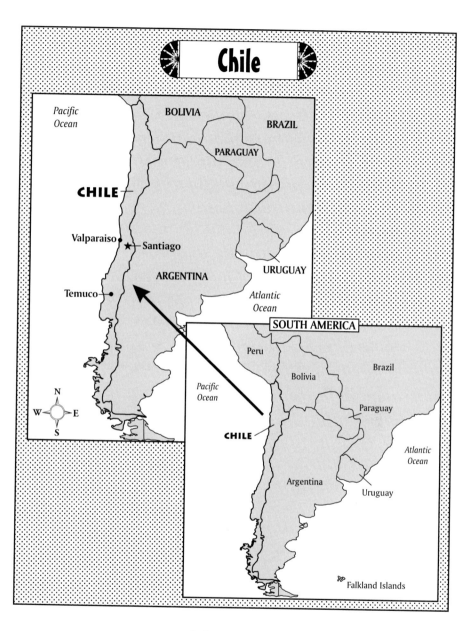

Map of Chile

Argentine government, at the request of Chile, was also hunting for him. His only chance for freedom was to leave South America, but as a fugitive he had no passport. Finally, his literary contacts came to his aid. A Guatemalan writer named Miguel Angel Asturias knew and admired Neruda for his poetry. Asturias, a diplomat for his country, was then on assignment in Argentina. He bore a slight resemblance to Neruda, so he suggested that Neruda use his passport to leave South America. Neruda agreed, and he successfully passed through checkpoints and boarded a ship for France. In his luggage, he carried the manuscript of a long poem he had been working on since he had visited the "lost city" of Machu Picchu in the Andes Mountains of Peru. Machu Picchu was an ancient city of the Inca Indians that had not been discovered until 1910, and it was almost perfectly preserved. The poem that Neruda wrote was no less than a history of Latin America and a memory of the peoples of South America, from the ancient Incas to the conquerors and immigrants from Europe.

Neruda had no idea if he would ever return to Chile, but he had written on the wall of his last hideout, " 'Goodbye, my country. I am leaving, but I take you with me.' "[5]

THE FOREST AND THE SEA

Pablo Neruda was the name he chose to use as the author of his books. His real name was Neftalí Ricardo Reyes Basoalto. He was born in Parral, a town in central Chile, on July 12, 1904. His father was José del Carmen Reyes, who worked as a conductor on the railroad. His mother, Doña Rosa Basoalto de Reyes, was a schoolteacher, but Neftalí had no memory of her. She had died of tuberculosis only a month after giving birth to him. Neftalí's father was soon remarried, to Doña Trinidad Candia Marverde, a wonderful woman whom Neftalí was to call "the guardian angel of my childhood."[1]

Neftalí's father moved the family to Temuco, a town in the southern part of Chile. This was then Chile's frontier, a cold region of rain-drenched forests and snow-capped mountains. It was a harsh land, but it had its beauties. Young Neftalí was fascinated with the wildlife that teemed in the forests, and he began collecting specimens of everything from beetles to birds' eggs. He was also drawn to the local peasants, who were descended from the first inhabitants of this harsh country. They wore long, black capes to protect them from the continual rain. He listened to their tales of the Araucanian Indians, who, centuries before, had been forced by the Spanish conquerors to retreat to this last outpost in the cold and forbidding South. The Araucanians fought not only the Spanish but also later waves of immigrants from the North. They were finally brought under control by the Chilean government forces in the late nineteenth century. This "superb race," as Neruda called the Araucanians, was virtually wiped out over the course of more than three hundred years, from 1540 to the 1880s.

Neftalí began school in 1910, in an old mansion that was poorly furnished. The hardy settlers of Temuco had more respect for hard work than for education, so there were few books in homes and the small library was seldom open. Nevertheless, books began to interest Neftalí, and he read of the adventures of

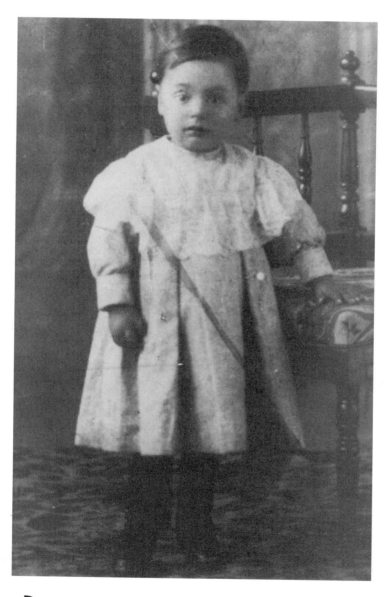

Pablo Neruda as an infant. He was baptized Naftalí Ricardo Reyes Basoalto.

U.S. showman Buffalo Bill and the accounts of famous travelers to all parts of the world.

A friend of Neftalí's fell in love with the town blacksmith's daughter, and he asked Neftalí to write love letters to her in his name. Neruda later recalled that these letters were probably his first literary efforts. The girl soon realized who had actually written the letters and to show her appreciation gave Neftalí a pear-shaped fruit called a quince, which he did not eat but saved. He continued writing letters to the girl on his own, and continued receiving quinces.

At about the age of nine, Neftalí began writing poetry. He did not know how it came about, but many years later, as an adult, he wrote:

> *Llegó la poesia*
> *a buscarme. No sé, no sé donde*
> *salió, de invierno o río,*
> *No sé cómo o cuándo*
>
> . . .
>
> *allí estaba sin rostro*
> *y me tocaba.*[2]

> [Poetry arrived
> searching for me. I don't know, I don't know where
> it rose from, from winter or a river,
> I don't know how or when
>
> . . .
>
> it was there, faceless
> and it touched me.]

best to keep his poems secret or at least unnoticed, but eventually they were revealed. He had an uncle named Orlando Masson who published a local journal in Temuco. Masson allowed Neftalí the run of his office, and the boy became acquainted with the smell of ink and newsprint. Masson became aware of Neftalí's literary talents and even published some of his earliest writings in his newspaper.[9]

Neftalí's father, instead of being pleased with his son's accomplishments, was angered. He did not approve of literary pursuits. He thought they were useless and of no help in the hard struggle to make a living in the harsh environment of southern Chile. He tried to lure his son away from poetry and literature by taking the boy along with him on his numerous trips for the railroad. Although Neftalí marveled at the variety and awesome beauty of the landscape through which they passed, these trips did not change his outlook. They merely increased his desire to put all of the things he saw and felt into words. This angered his father even more, and he threatened to punish the boy if he continued to waste his time reading and writing verses. Nevertheless, Neftalí sent some poems to the journal *Corre-Vuela* in the capital city of Santiago. One of them, "*Mis ojos*" (My eyes), was accepted for publication, and Neftalí, at the age of fourteen, became an acknowledged poet. During the following year, the journal printed more of his poems, and he won first prize in a poetry competition. None of this pleased his father.

Temuco was surrounded by mountains and dense forests, but not far to the west lay the sea. Neftalí longed to see this vast ocean, which he had read so much about in his travel books. When he was fifteen, his father was given the use of a house in the coastal town of Bajo Imperial. After another memorable train trip through the Chilean countryside, the family arrived in the village, which consisted of only a few houses strung along a river that led to the sea. "The first time I stood before the sea, I was overwhelmed," Neruda wrote later.[10] It was the beginning of a lifetime of devotion to the sea.

The streets of Bajo Imperial were filled with horses ridden by Chilean, German, and Araucanian riders who seemed to be a part of their mounts, half man and half horse. Neftalí soon began riding horses himself, and would spend long hours riding alone at the edge of the sea. He absorbed the images of pounding surf on one side and the towering mountains and tangled forests on the other. It was all stored in his memory and would find expression in his poetry, which he continued to write despite his father's strong objections.

To conceal his published writings from his father, Neftalí decided to change his name. He thought that a European name would be the least noticeable, so he chose the name of the Czech writer Jan Neruda, which he had come across in a literary magazine. He chose Pablo (Paul) perhaps because of his admiration for the French poets Paul Valéry and Paul Verlaine. For whatever reason, he signed his next poem "Pablo Neruda as of October 1920."[11]

After the family's return to Temuco, Neruda did his best to please his father, but he could not join in the activities of his schoolmates. He was not good at sports, and he was shy around girls. He preferred to take long walks alone or read in his room. On the coast, during one of his solitary rides, he had found a public library in the small town of Puerto Saavedra. There he met an old poet named Augusto Winter. Winter was impressed with Neruda's literary appetite, and he recommended several poets and dramatists such as the Norwegian dramatist Ibsen and the Argentine poet Vargas Vila. Neruda subsequently wrote that he "gobbled up everything, indiscriminately, like an ostrich."[12]

It is not clear how Neruda came to leave Temuco. Somehow he was given the chance to study in Santiago. Could it have been the influence of prominent citizens such as Orlando Masson or Gabriela Mistral? Neruda said only that "after many years of school, and the struggle through the math exam each December, I was outwardly prepared to face the university in Santiago."[13] He was going there to study French in preparation for a teaching career. To his father, the profession of teacher must have seemed an acceptable middle-class career, so he relented and allowed Neruda to leave for the capital city. Neruda was sixteen years old and already a published poet. He packed his trunk, donned his only suit, and took the train to Santiago:

> . . . *miré haci atrás*
> *llovía,*
> *se perdia mi infancia.*
> *Entró el Tren fragoroso*
> *en Santiago de Chile, capital,*
> *y ya perdí los árboles.*[14]

> [I looked backward,
> it was raining,
> my childhood was fading.
> The thundering train entered
> Santiago de Chile, the capital,
> and I had already lost my trees.]

FROM POET TO DIPLOMAT

Neruda arrived in Santiago in March 1921, when he was nearly seventeen years old. He quickly acquired a reputation as a brooding, solitary, and penniless poet. He dressed always in black, and wore a heavy railroad-man's cape, which had been given to him by his father. He took long walks alone through the streets of Santiago at night. He lived in a rooming house for students, which he later wrote, "meant starvation."[1] He ate little but wrote more, and soon became known in intellectual and literary circles. Fellow students at the Instituto Pedagócio copied his dress and mannerisms and began to quote lines from his poetry to one another. He won first prize in the student federation's poetry contest, and he wrote for student newspapers and founded his own journal. He was invited to read his poems in front of literary societies and even at popular festivals. He later declared that he had a terrible voice and had been laughed off the stage at the nonliterary events. "You starving poets! Get out! Don't spoil the celebration,"[2] the crowds shouted.

In 1923, he published his first book of poems, *Crepusculario* (Twilight book). Most of the poems had been written when he was sixteen and seventeen years old, and most were sad remembrances of youth and feelings of friendship and love. Poetry in Latin American countries holds a much more important place in popular culture than it does in most other countries. Any poet, published or not, can usually find an audience simply by reciting his or her poems at street fairs, festivals, or any other form of public entertainment. Schools and colleges have poetry contests, and most cities and states present awards for the best poetry presented in practically any medium. Neruda, now a published poet, was asked by student groups, magazine and newspaper editors, and producers of popular entertainments such as concerts or dances to read from his work. As a result, he soon became known to a wide range of people outside his circle of friends and fellow poets.

Pablo Neruda posed for this picture with his sister, Laura, shortly before his departure for Santiago.

A year later, in 1924, Neruda published his second book of poems, *Veinte poemas de amor y una canción desesperada* (Twenty poems of love and a song of despair), which was to become one of the most famous books of love poetry ever written. Neruda was often asked if the poems were directed to a specific person. He would say only that the poems were addressed to two women, whom he called Marisol and Marisombra. Marisol he identified with the country and the sea, with his life and love in Temuco. Marisombra he identified with the city, with the joys and sorrows of student life. He would not identify them further.[3]

The poems in *Veinte poemas de amor*, like all great love poetry, seemed private and personal, and yet any reader could imagine that they applied to himself or herself alone. Such unforgettable lines as *"Es tan corto el amor, y es tan largo el olvido"* (Love is so short, and forgetting is so long) or *"Inclinado en las tardes tiro mis tristes redes"* (Leaning into the evening I cast my sad nets) seemed to cry out for reciting or for singing. Indeed, many of the poems have long been favorites for poetry readings and have been set to music on both the popular and the concert music level in Europe and in the United States.

The book received attention throughout Latin America, not only among other poets but also among the larger public who did not usually read poetry. Young people recited his lines to one another, and older people marveled at the beauty of the lines that did not contain the traditional flowery speech and images they were used to. The Argentinean novelist Julio Cortázar has written about the effect of the book:

> Few knew Pablo Neruda, this poet who so suddenly returned us to what was ours, who pulled us from a vague theory of beloved ladies and European muses and placed us in the arms of a woman immediate and tangible. He showed us that the love of a Latin American poet could be given and written about . . . in the simple

words of the day, with the smell of our streets,
with the simplicity in which we could discover
beauty without having to agree to a grand purple
style and divine proportions.[4]

At the age of twenty, Neruda had become a major
voice in Chilean literature, and he decided to drop out
of school and devote himself full time to writing. When
his father learned of this decision, he promptly cut off
Neruda's modest allowance. From then on, Neruda
was on his own.

Unfortunately, Neruda's sudden lack of any income
came at the same time that the Chilean economy was
beginning a decline.

During World War I, Chile's natural resources such
as nitrates, which were used in the manufacture of
explosives, and copper had been in great demand.
When the war ended, there was little need for such
materials, particularly nitrates, so the country entered a
period of economic depression. Many people had
made great fortunes during the war years, and they
retained them. The ordinary workers, however, had
not been able to save up any wealth that they could
draw on in bad times. The gap between the rich and
the poor became wider than it had ever been. The rich,
of course, had more influence with the government, so
little help was given to the poor. This underclass of the
poor was known as *las rotas*, "the broken ones," which
described their condition well.

Pablo Neruda (seated with his arms folded) and a group of young poets in Santiago. Clearly, he is the center of the group.

Neruda and his friends from the university felt sympathy for *las rotas* and did everything they could to help them in their demands for equal rights and fair employment practices. In 1920, Arturo Alessandri Palma had been elected president of Chile on a program of reform. He had the backing of university students and liberal writers and intellectuals, as well as organized workers. Once in office, however, Palma found that he could not get his programs passed by the congress. Chile, like the United States, is a republic governed by a president and a legislature (congress). Chile, however, has many political parties, so a president, who is a member of one party, must have the support of other parties in addition to his own in order to gain a majority vote on any program he wants the congress to pass. Palma, who had been able to gain the support of enough parties to win the presidency, was not able to do the same to get his programs passed in the congress. He found it was impossible to go up against the well-to-do conservative parties that had helped him become president but who did not want to see his reforms made into law.[5]

When Palma failed to deliver his reforms, Neruda and his fellow intellectuals gave their support to the leader of the organized workers, Luis Emilio Recabarren, who became the founder of Chile's Communist party. Neruda contributed to Recabarren's movement by writing articles for antigovernment journals and by joining in street demonstrations. Sometimes he and his fellow demonstrators were beaten by the police who tried to break up their gatherings. Although Neruda did not suffer imprisonment or censorship at this time, the experience affected him deeply. "From that time on," wrote Neruda, "politics became part of my poetry and my life. In my poems I could not shut the door to the street, just as I could not shut the door to love, life, joy, or sadness in my young poet's heart."[6] He became a dedicated leftist, a person who works for reform or changes in the existing social or political system with the aim of creating greater personal freedom or improved economic conditions.

Despite his growing popularity as a poet, Neruda was still living in poverty. He was forced to move from lodging to lodging because he was unable to pay his rent. He often went hungry, and his anguish found reflection in his poetry. These were hard times, but they did not stifle his creativity, and he produced another book of poetry, a series of sketches, and even a short novel. All of this brought him to the attention of people outside Santiago's literary circle. These people were educated and well-off businessmen, lawyers, doctors, and government officials who read the latest magazines and journals and kept in touch with what was going on in their capital city.

Fortunately, Chile, as well as most other Latin American countries, encouraged its writers and artists by giving them diplomatic assignments throughout the world. The work was not difficult, and it gave the aspiring artist enough time and financial security to work at his or her craft. Actually, this was a form of government support for the arts, which most countries gave in outright grants of money. Through a friend, Neruda obtained a meeting with the head of the department in Chile's foreign ministry that was responsible for making these diplomatic assignments. This bureaucrat was familiar with Neruda's poetry and he chatted with him for an hour about literature and the arts. At the end of the conversation, the man told Neruda, "You may now consider yourself virtually appointed to a post abroad."[7] It turned out that the man was bored with his job and enjoyed talking with Neruda about the lively world of art and artists. They

Arturo Alessandri Palma, president of Chile from 1920 to 1924, failed to live up to Neruda's expectations.

met regularly to discuss Neruda's appointment, but each conversation would eventually turn to poetry and the arts.

This went on for two years, until one day Neruda ran into an old friend named Victor Bianchi. Bianchi came from a prominent family and had at one time served as an ambassador, so he knew how the foreign service worked. "Hasn't your appointment come through yet?" asked Bianchi. Neruda assured him that it would come through any day now, because a high official in the foreign ministry who loved the arts was working on his behalf. Bianchi said, "Let's go see the minister." The foreign minister, when he heard Neruda's story, pressed a buzzer and summoned the official, who was asked abruptly what posts were open. The official, who could not now turn the conversation into a discussion of music, poetry, and the arts, meekly listed the countries throughout the world where posts were waiting to be filled. Neruda caught one name that he had never heard of before: Rangoon. When the minister asked him where he wanted to go, he answered "Rangoon" without hesitating. The minister ordered the official to give Neruda the appointment, and it was done within a matter of minutes. The official was deprived of pleasant conversation, and Neruda was given the means of escaping his poverty.[8]

Neruda and his friend Bianchi tried to locate Rangoon on an old globe that was in the minister's office. They finally located it in Burma, in southeastern Asia, in a dented portion of the battered globe. Later, when Neruda met his artistic friends and told them of the good news, he had completely forgotten the name of the city to which he was being sent. He had to tell them that he was going to some place in the Orient that was a hole on the map.

TO THE FAR EAST AND BACK

Neruda left for the Far East in 1927, but he took the long way to get there. He departed from Santiago by boat on June 14, just a month short of his twenty-third birthday. Neruda had invited a friend of his, Rafael Alvaro Hinojosa, to accompany him. To pay for Hinojosa's way, the first thing Neruda did when they arrived in Buenos Aires, Argentina, was to cash in the first-class ticket Neruda had been given by the foreign ministry. With the money, he purchased two third-class tickets to Europe on the German ship *Baden*. Hinojosa was a fast-talking, elegantly dressed young man who spoke English and had lived in New York. He liked to believe that he was a superb businessman and was constantly coming up with schemes to make him and his friends millionaires. He may not have been the most practical traveling companion, but Neruda liked him and found him amusing.[1]

Their first stop after leaving South America was Lisbon, Portugal, where they feasted on delicious food and gazed in wonder at the crowded streets and the strange buildings. Their next stop was Madrid, a city in Spain that later was to play such a large part in Neruda's life. They barely stopped there before boarding a third-class coach for a long and uncomfortable train ride to Paris, France. Even Neruda, who was no stranger to trains and trainmen, said it was the sorriest train ride in the world.

When they reached Paris, they immediately became part of the Latin American community that had sprung up there. They did not meet or converse with any Frenchmen, even though Neruda had once intended to teach French and read and spoke it well. They spent most of their time among other South Americans who had come to Paris to study or to escape political oppression in their homelands. Neruda was disappointed with Paris, and was glad to leave for Marseilles and the Mediterranean. From there they went through the Suez Canal and into the Red Sea and the Indian Ocean.

The ship was not scheduled to stop at Rangoon, the capital of Burma, so they had to stay with it until it reached Shanghai, China. In Shanghai, Neruda and Hinojosa eagerly disembarked to sample some of Shanghai's famous nightlife. It was a weeknight and most of the nightclubs were empty except for a few Russian women who tried to get the nearly penniless friends to buy them champagne. After a disappointing evening, they took separate rickshaws back to their ship. A rickshaw is a two-wheeled vehicle, usually for one passenger, pulled by a man running between shafts, like a horse drawing a carriage. It was raining lightly, so a cloth was put over the top of the rickshaws, protecting Neruda and Hinojosa from the rain but also preventing them from seeing where they were going. Soon Neruda heard feet other than his driver's running alongside. The trip seemed unusually long, and when both rickshaws stopped, Neruda and Hinojosa found themselves in a deserted place far from the harbor. The two were immediately surrounded by seven or eight Chinese men who beat them and took all of the little money they had and most of their clothing. The robbers left them their papers and their passports, however. Neruda and Hinojoso walked toward the harbor and were helped by kind passersby to make their way back to the friendly surroundings of their shabby third-class cabin.

The ship proceeded to Japan, and in Yokohama they had to stay in a seamen's shelter, which was little more than a room with straw mattresses on the floor. They expected to find money from Chile waiting at the Chilean consulate, but the problem was how to get there. Luckily, a Spanish-speaking man from the Basque region in the north of Spain looked after them and they eventually reached the consulate. The consul general of Chile treated them in a haughty manner and offered no help. He had not heard of any money waiting for Neruda and dismissed them with the excuse that he was off to have tea at the Imperial Court. Neruda and Hinojosa hounded the consulate day after day, until it was finally discovered that the money had arrived in Yokohama before they did and had been sitting in the bank. The consul had been notified, but he had been much too busy trying to gain favor with the royal family of Japan to take notice of such a trivial matter. When Neruda received the money, they went to the best restaurant in Tokyo and made up for their near-starvation. They had just enough money left to pay for third-class tickets on a boat bound for Burma.

The two men ran into more trouble at their next stop, Singapore. They were almost completely out of money, and the Chilean consul refused to advance them any of the money that Neruda said was waiting for him in Rangoon. Neruda tried to convince him that it was in Chile's interest for him to arrive in Rangoon in time to take up his duties there. The consul finally did lend them the money, for which he charged interest, and they finally set sail for Burma. Neruda repaid the loan, but without the interest, as soon as he reached Rangoon and received the money that was waiting for him at the Chilean consulate.[2]

Rangoon was situated at the muddy mouth of the Irrawaddy River, which Neruda thought to be the most beautiful name of any river in the world. Over the city loomed the gold dome of the Shwe Dagon Pagoda, which was more than twenty-five hundred years old. The streets teemed with people dressed in strange and vividly colored apparel. Here Hinojosa was to leave Neruda. He was going to continue on through Asia until he eventually reached New York, where he was sure his fortune awaited him. Neruda, for his part, looked forward to the new life that awaited him in this strange and exotic city.

Burma was then a colony of England, and Neruda soon became part of the diplomatic community. This was part of the mainly British society of businessmen and colonial officials, and Neruda felt out of place and lonely. Ever since he had left Chile, he had continued with his writing. He sent regular "chronicles" to the Chilean publication *La Nación*, and his new poems were mailed to literary journals in Spain. Instead of being inspired by his new surroundings, Neruda became more withdrawn. His poetry took a new turn.

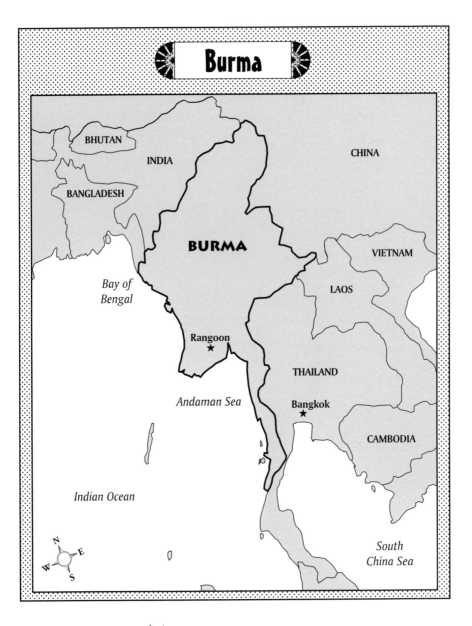

Map of Burma/Southeast Asia

His language, which formerly had been precise in his descriptions of nature and emotions, became almost mysterious with meanings that could not be easily understood by most casual readers. Loneliness and separation were the subjects of many of his poems of this period.

Neruda longed to absorb some of the spirit of the Orient and the ancient way of life of the multitudes surrounding him, but he was warned by his British friends not to become too friendly with the Burmese. If he did, he would be crossing the rigid class lines that separated the Burmese from the Europeans, and his status as a consul would be lowered. He ignored their warnings and became involved so deeply "into the soul and the life of the people"[3] that he fell in love with a native girl. She called herself Josie Bliss and she acted and dressed like an Englishwoman. In the privacy of the house they shared together, however, she donned native dress and used her Burmese name.

Unfortunately, it soon turned out that Neruda had made a mistake. Josie Bliss was possessive and jealous. She had a terrible temper and threw jealous tantrums even when Neruda received a letter or a telegram. She would admit no outsiders into their life together. Sometimes he would wake up at night to see her, dressed all in white, circling his bed with a knife in her hand. In the morning she would wait on him as though nothing had happened. "She would have ended up by killing me," Neruda wrote afterward.[4]

Fortunately, after a year in Burma, Neruda was transferred to Ceylon (now Sri Lanka), and he departed from Rangoon secretly. He left behind his clothing and his books and boarded the ship that would take him away from "the woman I lost and who lost me, because a volcano of anger boiled constantly in her blood."[5] Aboard ship, he began a new poem, "*Tango del viudo* (Widower's tango)," which was dedicated to Josie Bliss:

> *Así como me aflige pensar en el claro día de*
> *tus piernas . . .*
> > *y el perro de furia que asilas en el corazón,*
> > *así también veo las muertes que están entre*
> *nosotros*
> > *desde ahora,*
> > *y respiro en el aire la ceniza y lo destruido.*[6]
>
> [So it grieves me to think of the clear day
> of your legs . . .
> > and the furious dog you shelter in your heart,
> > and thus I also see the dead who are between us
> > from this day on,
> > and I breathe in the air the ashes of the
> destroyed.]

In later years, Neruda was to write two more poems about Josie Bliss in which he indicated that he had never forgotten her.

In Colombo, the capital of Ceylon, Neruda found the same social situation as in Burma. The English lived in their private compounds, attended their own churches, and spent their spare time in their own clubs waited on by an army of native servants. Surrounding them was the immense human mass of Asia. Neruda never felt at home in or accepted by either camp and experienced another period of intense loneliness. He lived in a bungalow in a suburb by the sea, where the familiar sound of crashing waves gave him some comfort. In the mornings he would stroll along the beach, watching the fisherman haul in their catch, and was appalled as he watched the natives massacre these shining creatures of the sea with their machetes. Sometimes he would come across elephants bathing in the sea. Neruda was fascinated by these huge creatures, who had been trained to do most of the heavy work in Ceylon. These were a far cry from the slow and clumsy creatures he had seen only in the zoo in Santiago.

To ease his loneliness, he acquired a dog and a pet mongoose to accompany him on his daily walks. The Asian mongoose is a slender, skunklike animal about thirty inches long from head to tail. Neruda's tame mongoose, whom he called Kiria, soon became a celebrity in his neighborhood. The mongoose is famous for its ability to kill or scare away deadly snakes. One day some children brought Neruda a large and deadly snake for his mongoose to battle with and subdue. Kiria took one look at the fierce snake and bolted for home. Much later, Neruda wrote sadly that in this way he lost the respect of his neighbors, "more than thirty years ago, in the suburb of Wellawatte."[7]

In 1929, Neruda made a trip from Ceylon to India to attend a meeting of the India National Congress Party. India was then beginning its long struggle against British rule of the huge country. The leader of this movement for independence was Mohandas K. Gandhi, who favored a policy of nonviolence toward the British. By refusing to engage in rioting or armed conflict, he won the admiration of the world and brought his people's plight under British rule to the attention of the outside world.

Neruda believed that Gandhi, despite his simple ways and humble mode of living, was a master politician and a shrewd, practical man. Neruda also met the Nehru family, who favored a more active campaign against the British but who, nonetheless, followed Gandhi's lead. The son, Jawaharlal Nehru, was later to become India's first prime minister after the country won its independence in 1947.

Neruda also met Subhas Chandra Bose, who, in contrast to Gandhi and the Nehrus, was a fiery speaker and protestor who favored violence against the imperialist British forces. During World War I, he had aided the Japanese when they invaded India. As a result, after the war he was tried for treason and condemned to death. After widespread protests and many legal battles, the British were forced to pardon him, and he became a popular hero to the masses. Neruda was very impressed with Bose, and his later political activities were undoubtedly influenced by Bose's example.

Back in Colombo, Josie Bliss suddenly showed up in front of Neruda's house. She had brought her own food and bedding with her and pitched her camp at his doorstep. She confronted anyone who approached Neruda's house, driving them away with her insults, and she even attacked a girl who had come to call on him. After a few weeks of this, the local police told Neruda that they would have to deport her if he did not take her in. Neruda did not dare to let her into his house. "She was a love-smitten terrorist, capable of anything," he later wrote.[8] Suddenly, she decided to go away, but she begged Neruda to accompany her to her ship. There she covered Neruda with kisses, even to his shoes. Neruda was shaken, and the scene remained burned in his memory. He could do nothing but let her go. He never saw her again.

Through all of this, Neruda was working on his poetry. One of his major works, *Residencia en la tierra* (Residence on earth), was written while he was in Burma and Ceylon. He asserted that his experiences in Asia had not influenced these poems, but their much wider view of the world and human experience must have been the result of his travels and residence abroad. Also, his loneliness had led him to read more often and more extensively than he had ever done before.

In 1930, Neruda received a surprise message from Chile's minister of foreign relations informing him that his term as consul in Colombo was ended and that he was being made consul to the British colony of Singapore and the Dutch colony of Batavia. Neruda took this to mean that he would receive two salaries, and that he could now afford to sleep in a bed instead of on a cot. When he left for Singapore, Neruda took with him a boy named Bhrampy who had done his housework in Colombo for a meager salary. Bhrampy managed to smuggle the mongoose Kiria past the customs inspectors along the way. They had to leave the dog behind with the villagers in Wellawatte.

When Neruda, Bhrampy, and Kiria arrived in Singapore, he registered at the elegant Raffles Hotel, ordered a cool drink, and sent Bhrampy out with his laundry for cleaning. When he tried to telephone the Chilean consulate, he learned that there wasn't any Chilean consulate in Singapore and that no one had ever heard of the previous consul. Neruda, who was just about broke, gathered up his still-wet laundry and Kiria, and he and Bhrampy made a dash for the ship that had brought them there. Luckily, the ship was still in the harbor, and they raced up the gangplank just in

Pablo Neruda (left) is shown relaxing on a beach in Rangoon, Burma, in 1927.

time. Neruda went back to the cabin that he had just left that morning and sank into bed exhausted. Such was his experience of Singapore.

When Neruda reached Batavia (now called Jakarta) on the island of Java, he was relieved to find that there was an actual Chilean consulate in the city. Upon arrival at the building, however, he found that it was already occupied by a grumpy Dutchman who said he was the consul. It seemed that the previous Chilean consul, a man named Mansilla, had never taken up his posts in Singapore or Batavia. Instead, he had hired the Dutchman to attend to his country's affairs and had gone off to Paris, where he lived on the fees that the Dutchman collected and sent to him. The Dutchman was furious because he had never been paid by Mansilla. Still, he must have managed to make some sort of living from the consulate, for he was not about to give it up to this young upstart from Ceylon.

After cabling Chile and explaining the situation to government officials, Neruda finally gained the right to take up his consular duties. These consisted of rubber-stamping invoices for goods shipped from Chile to the Dutch East Indies and collecting any fees required. He was barely able to make enough money to pay for his food and lodging, Bhrampy's small wages, and Kiria's upkeep. He described his life as "desperately uneventful."[9]

Kiria had grown much larger and was eating three or four eggs a day, and eggs were expensive in Java. She also started following Neruda wherever he went, even into the crowded and dangerous streets. One day he returned home to find her missing. She did not return the next day, and Neruda placed advertisements in the newspapers, but there were no replies. Kiria never returned. Bhrampy was ashamed that he had let the mongoose get out of the house and could not look Neruda in the eye. He felt so bad that he decided to return to Ceylon. Neruda did not like to see him go, but Kiria was the only thing the two had in common.

Neruda was now as alone as he had ever been, and when he met a local Dutch girl who was part Indonesian, he decided to marry her. The girl's name was Maria Antonieta Hagenaar Vogelzanz. "She was a tall, gentle girl and knew nothing of the world of arts and letters,"[10] Neruda wrote. She did not speak Spanish and he did not speak Dutch, so they spoke to each other in imperfect English. Maruca, as Neruda called her, was proud of being a consul's wife and went everywhere with him. Neruda wrote to his father and apologized for getting married without first asking his consent, but his father never replied. The son had disappointed his father once again.

SPAIN IN
THE HEART

In 1932, the Chilean government was facing a financial crisis and in an economy move shut down its consular posts in the Far East.[1] Neruda, with Maruca, returned to Chile, where he published two more books of poetry, *El hondero entusiasta* (The ardent slingsman) and *Residencía en la tierra* (Residence on earth). He had hoped to publish *Residencía*, which he considered his most important book so far, in Spain. His poems were well known there, and he thought that they would be better received by a knowledgeable Spanish audience. He was unable to find a Spanish publisher, however, so he agreed to publish a small edition of one hundred copies that were distributed to Chilean writers and intellectuals.

At that time, Chile, like the rest of the world, was suffering from an economic depression. Neruda was unable to earn enough from his writings to support himself and his wife, so he continued to work for the foreign ministry doing routine clerical tasks. Chile was then governed by a former army colonel, Carlos Ibáñez del Campo, who had been part of a military coup that took over the government in 1925 and was later appointed president. Neruda was disturbed by the political situation, so in 1933 he was glad to accept a consular post in neighboring Argentina. In Buenos Aires, Neruda was welcomed into literary circles and soon became acquainted with the leading poets and writers. There he met the Spanish poet and playwright Federico García Lorca, who was visiting Buenos Aires to direct one of his plays. Neruda and Lorca were often entertained together by artistic organizations and writers' groups. At one memorable dinner given in their honor by the international P.E.N. (poets, essayists, novelists) organization, they shared the podium and delivered a speech together, with one poet finishing a sentence the other had begun.

After less than a year in Buenos Aires, Neruda was transferred to Barcelona, Spain, to do the same sort of consular work that he had done in Argentina. This consisted of little more than adding columns of figures and rubber-stamping invoices and records of shipments to and from Chile. Neruda considered his superior, the consul general Tulio Maqueira, "the most dedicated official in the Chilean consular service." He was also one of the wisest, for he soon realized that Neruda was wasted in a job for which he had little liking and less talent. One day he said, "Pablo, you should go live in Madrid. That's where the poetry is."[2] So, with Maqueira's recommendation, Neruda became Chilean consul in the capital of Spain.

In Madrid, he quickly renewed his acquaintance with Lorca, and was introduced to the poet Rafael Alberti, who admired Neruda's poetry and had been reading poems from *Residencia* aloud to his friends. He helped Neruda settle into his new quarters. Neruda felt completely at home with his new friends, and his acceptance among them gave him a sense of security that he had never had before. He soon became part of the artistic and intellectual life of the city. He met with fellow poets, painters, architects, and sculptors who gathered every day in one or another's apartment or in the cafés of the city. The only shadows in this sunny world were the political situation in Spain and Neruda's growing estrangement from his unartistic and non-Spanish-speaking wife.

In 1935, Spain was going through a period of political unrest. The country had been governed for most of its history by a royal family in close alliance with the

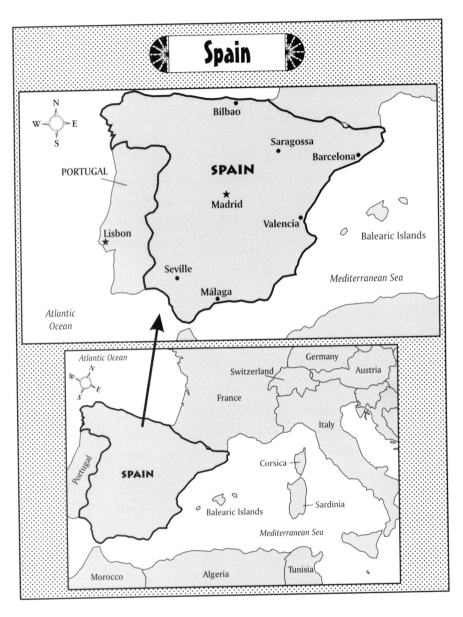

Map of Spain

Catholic Church and the country's wealthiest families. With the increasing hard times brought about by the worldwide economic depression, many people in the middle and lower classes began to call upon the government to do something to help the suffering masses. When the government failed to do anything, the people's objections took the form of protest meetings and strikes. Many of the more radical members of the working classes began to call for a complete change of government. Faced with growing unrest that threatened to turn into violence, King Alfonso XIII decided to step down and allow the formation of a republican form of government. This immediately divided the country into two opposing camps. One favored the return of the monarchy and the abolition of the few reforms that had been made by the government, and the other called for even more drastic changes toward a more democratic government and a freer society.

Neruda and his artistic and intellectual friends were wholeheartedly on the side of the new republic. In their speeches, their writings, and their teachings they resisted any attempts to bring back the monarchy. Neruda became very active in these activities, and was seldom at home. He became the editor of a literary review called *Caballo verde* (Green horse), which published new and revolutionary poetry. During all of this, Neruda's wife, Maruca, was on the sidelines. She still could not speak Spanish and was unable to find work.

Since Neruda seldom had enough money to pay his bills or household expenses, the burden on Maruca to make ends meet was becoming greater and greater. Despite all of this, Neruda and Maruca had a child whom they named Malva Marina. Unfortunately, she was born prematurely and suffered from Down's syndrome, a form of mental retardation, and was never a healthy baby.[3] This put another strain on the couple's relationship.

In addition, Neruda had met an older woman, the Argentine painter Delia del Carril. She was fifty years old, some twenty years older than Neruda, and an attractive and fascinating woman. She came from a wealthy Argentine family and as a child had a passion for horses. Later, as a painter, she would depict nothing but horses, sometimes giving them almost human form. She was a worldly woman who had been married and divorced, had lived in Paris among artists and writers, and had come to Spain to join in the exciting life of the new republic. She was different from any woman Neruda had ever known, and he was immediately attracted to her. She recognized Neruda as a fellow artist and was equally attracted to him. They became almost constant companions.[4]

For a while it seemed as though the Popular Front, as the supporters of the republic were called, had won in their struggle to achieve reform in the government. They had managed get some social programs passed and had done much to help poor farmers gain

The Royal Palace, built in the 1700s, was home to the Spanish royal family until 1931, when King Alfonso XIII was forced to leave the country. Neruda and his friends were on the side of the new republic and urged resistance to bringing back the monarchy.

ownership of the land they worked on. However, on July 17, 1936, a series of military revolts occurred in the Spanish colony of Morocco and in Spain itself. The army, with the backing of the monarchists and landowners, was attempting to wrest control of the government from the Popular Front. One of the leaders of the revolt in Morocco was General Francisco Franco. The Spanish civil war had begun, and was to continue for the next three years.

The war was brought home to Neruda when he learned that his good friend Federico García Lorca had been executed in southern Spain. Two days after the revolts had begun, Lorca went south to his native Andalusia, a section of Spain that was being overrun by the monarchist forces. Perhaps he wanted to join in the resistance, or perhaps he wanted to be a witness to what was happening in his native land. Whatever his reasons, he was caught and executed as an enemy of the Nationalists, as the rebels were called. For Neruda, Lorca's death was the greatest tragedy of the war. "And so the Spanish war, which changed my poetry, began for me with a poet's disappearance,"[5] he wrote. From then on, Neruda's poetry and writings would be more political and would speak for the underdog, the oppressed, and the powerless.

Neruda became an open and active supporter of the Republican cause. This brought him criticism from his superiors in the foreign ministry, who said that since Chile was neutral in the war, its diplomats had no business taking sides in public. Neruda responded by writing a series of poems, *España en el corazón* (Spain in the heart), in which he openly attacked the generals and the leaders of the Nationalists. Neruda's friends had all joined the Republican forces and were either fighting at the front or had withdrawn from Madrid in the face of the oncoming Nationalists, so his poems could not be published in the normal manner. The poet and printer Manuel Altaguirre had taken his printing presses with him and set them up behind the battle lines in eastern Spain. There he taught some soldiers to set type, and he set Neruda's poems into type as soon as he received them through friendly sources in Madrid. He had no paper on hand, so he and his soldiers had to make it themselves at an abandoned mill from any cloth or used paper they could find. Included in the mixture was an enemy flag and the bloodstained shirt of a captured enemy soldier. The book was printed and bound by hand and was widely distributed among Republican soldiers, who often carried it into battle in knapsacks and packs. As the Nationalists advanced, any copies of the book they found on dead or captured Republicans were destroyed. There are now only a few copies of the book left, one of which is preserved in the Library of Congress in Washington, D.C.

Because of his poems and his active support of the Republicans, Neruda was removed from his post as Chilean consul in Madrid. With his wife and daughter, he left for Valencia, in eastern Spain, where the Republican government had relocated. By this time many volunteers from other countries, including the United States, had come to Spain and had joined the Republican forces. They were called the International Brigades, and Neruda had seen many of them arrive in Madrid. Further support was needed, however, in the form of food and supplies, and committees sprang up in all of the major cities of Europe and the United States to help the cause of the Republicans. Neruda decided to go to Paris to help organize all of these committees into an international support system. This finally proved to be too much for his wife, and she departed with their daughter for her home in the Netherlands. Malva Marina would die in 1942 at the age of eight because of illnesses brought about by Down's syndrome.

In Paris, Neruda lived for a time with his friend Rafael Alberti, who had also helped Neruda when he first arrived in Madrid. After Maruca divorced him, Neruda married Delia del Carril and together they moved into a hotel in one of the poorer sections of Paris. He no longer had a consular position, so he was forced to take a job with his new friend, the poet Louis Aragon, who had formed an organization for the defense of culture. It was rumored in Paris that Delia, because of her family background, was a wealthy landowner and was supporting Neruda. Actually she was as poor as he was, and at times they barely had enough to eat. Neruda could not afford even to have his shoes repaired.

Neruda's main activity in Paris was to organize the International Writers' Congress to demonstrate the solidarity of the world's greatest authors in their support of the Spanish Republic. To make the point even

Pablo Neruda was advised to move to Madrid, which had a thriving artistic community. This monument in Madrid was built in honor of Miguel de Cervantes, the premier writer in Spanish literature. The figures in the foreground depict the central characters of Cervantes' masterpiece *Don Quixote*.

stronger, the congress was to be held in Madrid, which was still under attack by Nationalist forces. Neruda and his friends wrote to writers and intellectuals throughout the West, and the response was greater than anyone had expected. Notable writers from throughout the Western world agreed to attend, and those who could not sent their support. The Spanish Republican government came through with a large grant of money to cover the expenses for the congress and even to pay for the fares of delegates from other countries. A group of writers gathered in Paris and then took a train to Madrid. "Never had a train left Paris packed with so many writers," Neruda wrote later.[6]

The congress was attended by Stephen Spender from England, Ilya Ehrenburg from Russia, André Malraux from France, Octavio Paz from Mexico, and many more from other countries. Fighting was going on in some quarters of the city, but Neruda decided to visit his old home, which was near the front lines. He found the place a shambles, but looters had left most of his books and household possessions. Curiously, they had taken away his formal tail coat and his collection of Polynesian masks and Oriental knives that he had picked up in the Far East. He left everything as it was and returned to the congress.

The congress was a success but did little to gain the support of the rest of the world. The Republicans were mostly communists or socialists, and most countries were more wary of them than they were of the Fascists, as the Nationalists were beginning to be called. Madrid fell to the Nationalists in 1937, and the Republicans were eventually defeated in 1939. General Franco became head of the new government, which he promptly turned into a dictatorship that was to last more than thirty years.

Neruda returned to Chile in October 1937, just a few months after the writers' congress. He had not seen his father since 1933, and now his father was dying. If Neruda had hoped for some sort of acceptance or forgiveness from him, it was not forthcoming. Years later, Neruda wrote of his difficult father:

Mi pobre padre duro

. . .

un día con más lluvia que otros dias
el conductor José del Carmen Reyes
subió al tren de la muerte y hasta ahora no ha vuelto.[7]

[My poor, hard father

. . .

one day with more rain than other days
the conductor José del Carmen Reyes
climbed on the train of death and has not come back yet.]

Neruda threw himself into his work, determined to write a new poetry that would reflect his experiences in

Spain and would somehow serve his fellow man. He began to work on his *Canto general* (General song). "I felt a pressing need," he wrote in his *Memoirs*, "to write a central poem that would bring together the historical events, the geographical situations, the life and struggles of our peoples."[8] By peoples he meant all of the races and nationalities that had existed on the American continents since the beginning of time. Neruda was familiar with the work of the American poet Walt Whitman,[9] and he intended his work to be as broad and all-inclusive as Whitman's *Leaves of Grass*. For such an ambitious project he needed time, money, and a place to work undisturbed. He had the time, but the money was lacking. He submitted his idea to a publisher but was turned down. In the meantime, he had found the place he wanted—a stone house facing the sea in a place called Isla Negra. He found another publisher who was able to advance him some money, but it was to be paid directly to the owner of the house. Neruda moved into his new house immediately. "Isla Negra's wild coastal strip, with its turbulent ocean, was the place to give myself passionately to the writing of my new song,"[10] he wrote.

He had scarcely settled in his new home when he was called away. "Chile's Popular Front government decided to send me to France on the noblest mission I have ever undertaken,"[11] he wrote. More than a half million Spanish Republicans had fled into France to escape from Franco's armies. The unsympathetic French government herded them into concentration camps or shipped them to its colonies in North Africa.

Chile, alarmed at the happenings in Spain, had elected a more progressive government, and a Popular Front, similar to the one in Spain, had been formed. President Pedro Aguirre Cerda asked Neruda to go to France to see what he could do about getting Spaniards out of France and sent to Chile. "[B]ring me thousands of Spaniards," he told Neruda. "We have work for all of them."[12]

Neruda departed for Paris joyfully, even though he was in ill health after having recovered from an operation. He was suffering from phlebitis, an inflammation of the veins in one of his legs, that had made surgery necessary. In Paris, he ran into opposition from the old-line diplomats who were in charge. They did everything they could to discourage Neruda from carrying out his mission, but he forged ahead. He organized, screened, and selected the refugees who would be sent to Chile. The Spanish Republican government in exile bought a ship, the *Winnepeg*, and after further frustrating delays, more than two thousand immigrants were put aboard and sent on their way to a new life in Chile. Neruda was filled with pride. He later said that it was "the crowning point of my life."[13]

CHAPTER SIX

THE HEIGHTS OF MACHU PICCHU

 In 1939, the German army invaded Poland, and England and France quickly declared war on Germany. World War II had begun. Neruda was still in Paris, and watched from his window as the first French troops left for the front. He had seen this all before in Spain, and it depressed him. Since there was nothing left for him to do in Europe, he left for home.

The Chilean government was impressed with the way Neruda had handled the Spanish refugee problem. Here was a poet who could get things done. It rewarded him by making him consul general in

Mexico, and he and his wife moved to Mexico City in 1940. This was a most desirable post for Neruda, for the people of Mexico were engaged in the same social struggle that had failed in Spain. Reformers were calling for greater integration of the Indian population into the state, for the redistribution of land, and for the general betterment of the lives of the underprivileged. Neruda met and became friends with Mexico's great artists Diego Rivera, José Clemente Orozco, and David Alfaro Siqueiros. They were all engaged in the social struggle and were in constant trouble with the authorities. Siqueiros had even been sent to prison for his political activities. Neruda visited him in jail and together they planned his escape. Siqueiros was allowed to leave the prison in the company of his jailers and would return alone at night. Neruda personally arranged for a special visa to be attached to Siqueiros's passport, and the painter simply left for Chile. Neruda was suspended from his consulship for a month without pay for his part in the affair.[1]

Neruda continued to participate in activities that were not part of his duties as consul. Mexico in 1940 was changing from a revolutionary society to a conservative one that saw nothing wrong with great differences between the social classes. As usual in such a situation, the common people were at the bottom. Neruda continued to support those Mexicans who were pressing for reforms, and he attended mass demonstrations and meetings of workers. He was also outspoken in his support of the Soviet Union, which was then in a desperate struggle with Nazi Germany. Mexico and the United States were then still neutral in World War II, and not everyone was on the side of the Allies. In December 1941, Neruda was attacked by pro-German thugs while he was expressing his admiration for the Allied cause. He was beaten so badly that he had to be taken to a hospital for doctors to stitch up a four-inch cut on his head.[2] During his free time, he visited as many countries as he could in Central and South America. In his poetry, he tried to speak for all of Latin America in his concern for the inequalities in the social and political systems of the various countries. Social reforms had failed in Europe and Mexico, but he felt that there was still hope for South America.

Neruda was becoming frustrated with his country's conservatism and its disapproval of his activities. When he started a magazine called *Araucania*, named in honor of the Araucanian Indians he had known and admired in childhood, he received a dressing-down from his foreign minister. The government of Chile did not approve of a publication that seemed to picture the country as being populated by "backward" Indians. Neruda was also becoming more and more displeased with Mexico, which he felt had turned its back on the artists and workers who were so committed to social justice. In 1943, some Mexican factory workers went on a strike that lasted far longer than they had expected. When a group of strikers' wives organized a peaceful march on the presidential palace to bring attention to their hardships, they were fired upon by the guards and six or seven women were killed. When this outrage failed to arouse any response in the Mexican press, the congress, or even the labor unions, Neruda was disgusted. He decided to resign his consulship and return to Chile.

Before Neruda left Mexico, he was honored at a dinner attended by almost three thousand people. The president of Mexico sent his congratulations to Neruda on the job he had done as consul. This was the same president who had refused to hear the striking workers' wives, or perhaps had not even been told about them. Neruda considered him an insensitive and careless ruler, completely cut off from his people. Neruda later referred to him as an Aztec, after the ancient rulers of Mexico who, although creating a great civilization, made human sacrifices to ensure their favor with the gods.[3]

On his way home to Chile, Neruda visited Panama and Bolivia, where he gave readings of his poetry. He was impressed by the enthusiastic response of the people and began to identify with them as part of the whole South American continent. They all had the same heritage and roots. He spoke to them of their common culture that was unlike that of Europe or Asia and should be pursued independently. In Peru, he visited the ruins of the ancient Inca city of Machu Picchu, which was to make a deep and lasting impression on him.

Machu Picchu was built by the Incas of South America, probably in the fifteenth century. The Inca empire extended all the way from what is now Ecuador into Peru and Chile. Machu Picchu was built more than ten thousand feet above the Urubamba River, either as a fortress or as a center of some religious activity. It may simply have been a populated city situated safely above an unfriendly native population. Lying between two high mountains, Machu Picchu must have been almost impossible to attack or besiege. It is built entirely of huge stones fitted together so exactly that no cement or any other material was required to bind them together. The force of gravity was all that was needed to keep them in place. One of the architectural wonders of the world, it had lain abandoned for hundreds of years until it was discovered in 1911. The inhabitants must have fled during the Spanish conquest in the sixteenth century. The Spanish soldiers had never discovered it, and it had remained unknown for centuries because of the fact that the Inca civilization had no written records.

When Neruda visited Machu Picchu, he had to make the long climb up to it by horseback and on foot. Today, there are tourist buses and a railroad to take visitors to the ruins. But when Neruda saw them in 1943, they were still in a condition close to their original state. In his most famous poem, *"Alturas de Macchu Picchu"* (The heights of Machu Picchu), which was to become part of his *Canto general*, Neruda wrote:

> *Entonces en la escala de la tierra he subido*
> *entre la altroz maraña de las selvas perdidas*
> *hasta ti, Macchu Picchu.*
> *Alta ciudad de piedras escalares,*
> *por fin morada del que lo terrestre*
> *no escondió en las dormidas vestiduras.*
> *En ti, como des lineas paralelas,*
> *la cuna del relámpago y del hombre*
> *se macían en un viento de espinas.*[4]

[Then on the ladder of the earth I climbed
through the savage thicket of lost forests
up to you, Machu Picchu.
Lofty city of laddered stone,
finally the dwelling of him the earth
had not hidden in her sleeping vestments.
In you, like two parallel lines,
the cradles of lightning and of man
move in a wind of thorns.]

As he stood on the heights overlooking the spectacle, he had a revelation: "I felt Chilean, Peruvian, American. On those difficult heights, among those glorious, scattered ruins, I had found the principles of faith I needed to continue my poetry."[5]

The ruins of Machu Picchu, an ancient city that lay undiscovered until 1911, are in Peru.

By the time he returned to Chile, Neruda was an ardent supporter of political reform and change in the social structure of his country. He threw himself into politics and campaigned for the Popular Front, backing the liberal president Juan Antonio Ríos. When the Popular Front's more radical parties won control of the legislature, Ríos became fearful that the more moderate members would desert him. He refused to cooperate in passing the sweeping reforms called for by the radicals. Ríos and the moderates also hesitated in joining the United States, Great Britain, and the Soviet Union in their war against Germany and Japan. This infuriated Neruda, who was filled with admiration for the people of the Soviet Union in their battle to defend their homeland against the invading Germans.

Neruda had hoped to settle down in Isla Negra and continue work on his *Canto general*, but he was constantly called upon to address political meetings and to read his poetry in public. He was tremendously popular with the people, particularly with the working classes, with whom he identified. He became so disheartened with the political situation in Chile, where the elected officials seemed to do nothing to lessen the gap between the rich and the poor, that he decided to run for the Senate on his platform of social reform, which included greater recognition of the rights of the Indian population and a betterment of conditions for the workers in the copper and nitrate mines. In the election of 1945, he easily won, and then took his seat as a member of the Communist party.[6] He chose the Communists because they seemed to be the only party in Chile that had the support of the people and the power to get things done. He had always admired the Soviet Union and had become friends with the many European intellectuals who were openly Communist.

Unfortunately, this brought him into opposition with the moderate and conservative elements in Chile and with the anticommunist governments of the West. The Cold War was just beginning, and throughout its course Neruda would remain a staunch Communist.

Neruda had drawn most of his support from the workers in the great mining districts of Chile. There, the corporations who owned the nitrate and copper mines ruled almost as separate governments, even printing their own money and maintaining their own armies of security police. They banned political parties and public assembly of any kind and did not allow a free press. Neruda often visited these regions and tried to explain to the workers what their situation was and what they could do to improve it under the law. This brought him into open conflict with the army, which was completely on the side of the corporations. At one point Neruda was confronted with an army tank that parked directly in front of him as he spoke, its commander staring at him from the gun turret. Neruda went on speaking and finished what he had to say. The tank commander did nothing, but the threat was there for all to see.

Neruda and his fellow reformers were able to accomplish little in the Senate. Members of the opposition, who were all skilled politicians, prevented the reformers' proposals from reaching the Senate floor by launching a barrage of flowery speeches. Neruda felt frustrated until, in 1946, a new candidate for president arose who promised to see that reforms were carried out and that help was given to the workers and peasants. His name was González Videla, and Neruda was so impressed by him that he became his campaign manager. Neruda traveled throughout the country, carrying the message of Videla's promises. Videla won the election in a landslide victory, but once in office began to abandon his backers and friends. He quickly became one of the "aristocracy" of Chile and ignored the pleas for help from the lower classes who had elected him. He encouraged investment in Chilean industry, using resources from the United States, but did little with the added wealth to ease the plight of the workers in the copper and nitrate mining companies. When Neruda and his comrades complained and began condemning him publicly, Videla ordered the arrest of all those who spoke against him. He also clamped down on the press, imposing a strict censorship. Neruda replied to this with an open letter published in a prominent journal in Venezuela in which he fiercely attacked Videla and his policies. His speeches in the Senate became more critical of the government, and Videla's supporters began calling for his dismissal. Videla finally ordered Neruda's arrest, and the poet had no choice but to go underground. Arrest would have meant either imprisonment in one of the special stockades in the Chilean desert built for political prisoners or even death. Neruda began moving from house to house, sheltered by his friends. A little more than a year later, in February 1949, he was smuggled across the Andes Mountains into Argentina, where he managed to obtain passage to Paris. His years of exile had begun.

EXILE AND
RETURN

When Neruda arrived in Paris in 1949, he was still using his friend Miguel Angel Asturias's passport to travel, which he felt duty bound to return. Neruda had many friends in Paris, and they advised him to check into the elegant George V Hotel, where people were usually not asked to show their passports. Word got around Paris of Neruda's problem and help soon arrived in the figure of the great painter Pablo Picasso.

Picasso was a Spaniard who had lived in Paris for most of his life, and he was familiar with Neruda's poetry and with his political problems. Neruda was an illegal alien traveling under someone else's passport, and the French press had reported that he was in Paris. Picasso used his influence with the French authorities to allow Neruda to remain in France.[1] Through a friend in the Chilean embassy, Neruda managed to get his passport renewed, but the Chilean government continued to harass him. It did not want him returned home by force, but it did not seem to want him to be comfortable anywhere else either. When a Chilean official asked the police to take away Neruda's passport, the chief of police refused on the grounds that it was a valid passport, no matter how it had been renewed. He told Neruda that someone "seems to be your determined enemy. But you can stay in France as long as you wish."[2]

Neruda learned that there was a file on him in the French Ministry of Foreign Relations. It reported that Neruda and his wife, Delia del Carril, traveled to and from Spain carrying important messages to the Republicans from the Soviet Union. The Nerudas supposedly communicated with the Soviet Union through the famous Soviet writer and journalist Ilya Ehrenburg. Neruda had not been to Spain since the civil war there and had never met Ehrenburg, so this false information was probably the work of an enemy in the Chilean embassy. Since he was supposed to be so close to Ehrenburg, Neruda decided to go to meet the celebrated journalist himself. He went directly to Ehrenburg's apartment and introduced himself as his supposed great friend Pablo Neruda. Ehrenburg was momentarily confused, but then replied that he knew Neruda's poetry and had wanted to meet him, but first Neruda must try some of the excellent sausage he was having for lunch.[3] The two became great friends, and Neruda's admiration and affection for the Soviet Union increased.

Neruda was in great demand as a speaker and as a reader of his own poems. His troubles with the Chilean government were now well known, and he was admired throughout Europe as a defiant challenger of unjust authority. When he was invited by the Union of Soviet Writers to visit the Soviet Union in 1949, he eagerly accepted. The occasion was the 150th anniversary of the birth of Russia's greatest poet, Alexander Pushkin, and Neruda was honored to be associated with the event. The Union of Soviet Writers also invited him to a congress where he met many famous and new Soviet writers and renewed his acquaintance with Ehrenburg. He traveled throughout the Soviet Union and was immensely impressed with the people and the vastness of the land. He was now a confirmed Communist and Soviet sympathizer, which continued to make him unpopular with the governments of the West. The readers and writers of poetry, however, hailed him as a world master.

Even though he had become a world traveler and lecturer, Neruda had continued work on his huge poem *Canto general*, which he had begun in 1939. In 1950, it was published in Mexico and was immediately banned in Chile. In addition to his masterpiece "*Alturas de Macchu Picchu*," it contained attacks on President Videla and United States corporations, particularly the United Fruit Company, which controlled so much of the economies of Central and South American countries. The book was circulated in an underground edition, however, and it became famous in Chile as well as around the world. Like all of Neruda's works, it was immediately translated into all the major languages.

During his stay in Mexico, Neruda had met a woman who was to have a great influence on him for the rest of his life and to whom most of his nonpolitical poetry was dedicated. Her name was Matilde Urrutia, and she became his constant companion, traveling with him to India, China, and Italy. Neruda was still married to Delia del Carril, but his life of exile and his almost constant traveling had caused them to drift apart.

In Italy, Neruda was greeted enthusiastically wherever he went and was invited to read his poems everywhere—at universities, in museums, in palaces, and even to the workers on the docks in Genoa. The Italian government, however, was not so welcoming,

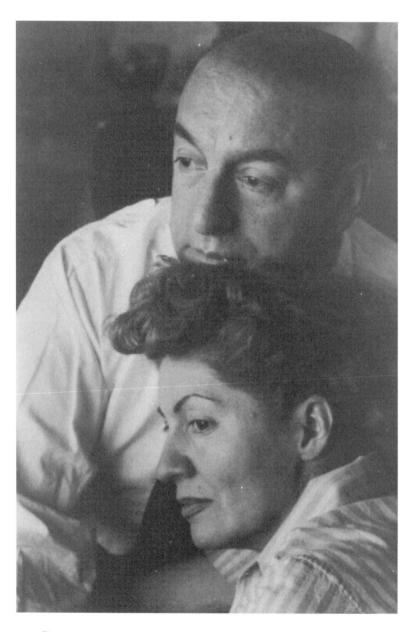

Pablo Neruda met his third wife, Matilde Urrutia, in Mexico.

and he was followed constantly by police. Neruda thought that this was because his poetry was so radical and in favor of the people's struggles, but it turned out that the Chilean government was bringing a great deal of pressure on the Italian government to expel him from the country. Neruda was offered sanctuary in a villa on the beautiful island of Capri. The owner was an Italian historian who was enraged over his country's treatment of Neruda. On Capri, Neruda and Matilde led a dreamlike existence, taking long walks among the orchards and vineyards and along the rocks of the coast, away from the tourists who thronged to the island during the summer.

On Capri, Neruda completed his next book of poems, *Los versos del capitán* (The captain's verses). It was published in Naples in 1952, without Neruda's name on the cover or title page. Many who knew that Neruda was the author assumed that he had hesitated to put his name on it because it would embarrass the Communist party. The book was a series of passionate love poems that expressed his devotion to Matilde Urrutia. At that time Neruda was a chief spokesman for Communist artists and writers, and he regularly appeared at party conferences, congresses, and award ceremonies. The only passion the party recognized was for the cause of communism and world peace on Soviet terms. Neruda, however, later explained that he did not acknowledge the poems because they would have caused pain to Delia del Carril, from whom he was now separated but still had a great deal of affection for.[4]

In 1952, Carlos Ibáñez was about to be elected president of Chile. This was the same Carlos Ibáñez who had been made president after the coup in 1925. This time around, Ibáñez put himself forward as a national reformer and declared the harsh policies of Videla's presidency would be relaxed.[5] He also made it clear that one of the first things he would do was cancel the order for Neruda's arrest. Neruda was now free to return to his homeland, which he did on August 12, with Matilde at his side. He was welcomed home with great warmth, not only by his fellow poets and artists but also by the general public, who had never forgotten him.

HONORS, HOPE, AND DESPAIR

In his *Memoirs*, Neruda says that during the next five years nothing out of the ordinary happened to him. Yet he published a new book of poems and began or continued work on three others. He also organized the Continental Congress of Culture that was held in Santiago and attracted artists and writers from all over the Americas. In 1954, he was honored on his fiftieth birthday by writers from all over the world who came to Santiago to congratulate him. That same year he divorced his wife of eighteen years, Delia del Carril. "Sweetest of consorts," he called her, "thread of steel and honey to me during the years when my poetry sang most, [who] was my perfect mate for eighteen years."[1] He had decided to marry Matilde Urrutia, and his often confused personal and emotional life now seemed to be settling into a pattern of domestic peace.

Neruda and Matilde moved into a new house in Santiago that was conveniently situated next to the city zoo. Neruda visited the zoo often, taking pleasure in the rare animals he depicted often in his poetry. He also owned a home in Valparaíso, a seaside city near Santiago that had fascinated Neruda while he had been a student back in the 1920s. His home in Isla Negra continued to be his retreat where he could enjoy moments of solitude and gain renewed inspiration and vigor from his closeness to the sea. All of these homes were crowded with Neruda's collections of books, artifacts, and seashells that he had gathered during his years of travel.

Neruda had always been an avid collector of anything unusual that caught his interest. One of his earliest interests was in seashells, which he had begun picking up on the beach when he was a child. In the Far East and in Mexico he had roamed the beaches to find rare and exotic specimens that he either shipped home or carried with him to new posts. Like all collectors, he traded, purchased, accepted as gifts, and even swiped ("there's no such thing as an honest collector,"[2] he wrote) pieces to add to his collections. When the famous English botanist Sir Julian Huxley visited Chile, he asked to meet Neruda. He was taken to Neruda's house and when the two men were introduced to each other, Huxley said frankly, "I'm more interested in you as a shell collector than as a poet."[3] The two went off happily to view Neruda's collection. They talked with ease, using the Latin names for the thousands of shells that were on display throughout the house.

In 1952, Neruda had been awarded the Stalin Peace Prize, one of the highest honors that the Soviet Union could bestow. Every year after that, Neruda returned to the Soviet Union to act as a judge for the award. He used these trips to revisit the scenes of his youth in Europe and the Far East and to give readings of his poetry wherever he went. He picked up awards and literary prizes from almost every country he visited. His poetic output, which had always been remarkable, continued at such a rate that publishers could hardly keep up with him. In 1962, the millionth copy of his youthful work *Veinte poemas de amor* was printed, an astonishing number for a single book of poems. His other books continued to sell throughout the world in numbers far greater than those for any other poetic works of the century. With such recognition and such acclaim it was expected that Neruda would be awarded the Nobel Prize in Literature, and

Pablo Neruda and his wife, Matilde, in their home in Valparaíso, Chile. The carousel horse is part of one of Neruda's collections of unusual items.

every year rumors began circulating in the literary world that he was about to be chosen. In 1961, it looked as though his time had finally come, and Neruda prepared to make the trip to Stockholm, Sweden, to receive the prize. However, the Swedish Academy, which awards the prize, decided on the Greek poet George Sefaris, and Neruda returned to his writing, collecting, and traveling. In 1964, the French philosopher, writer, and playwright Jean-Paul Sartre was awarded the prize but turned it down for political and personal reasons. When he announced his decision, he said that the prize should have gone to Neruda anyway. As a result of Sartre's refusal, however, no prize for literature was awarded that year.

Neruda had never visited the United States, although his poetry was read and admired there by fellow poets and practically all serious readers of poetry. The main reason for this was that since the end of World War II the United States and the Soviet Union had been engaged in a bitter Cold War that had divided most of the world into two opposing systems of government: democracy and communism. The threat of war between the two major powers was always present, and each of them was suspicious and mistrustful of anyone who sympathized with the other. Neruda was almost alone among Western writers and intellectuals who still believed in the ideals of the Communist party. After the death of the Soviet dictator Joseph

Stalin in 1953, the new head of the Soviet Union, Nikita Khrushchev, had revealed to the world the horrible atrocities that had been committed by the Stalin regime during the years it had been in power. Thousands upon thousands of people had been executed or condemned to prison or exile in Siberia because of their opposing political beliefs or simply because they did not agree with a particular policy of the government. Neruda had taken the position that these atrocities were a sideline in the march for social justice and not the result of flaws in the communistic system. Many former Communists had turned away from the party and now actively opposed it, but Neruda continued to believe and act as if communism were the only system that could achieve universal equality. In addition, Neruda had never ceased to criticize in his poetry and in his speeches the gigantic American corporations he believed had plundered Latin America of its wealth and had practically enslaved its workers. With such a background, it was no surprise that Neruda was not welcomed by the United States government or its conservative spokespeople in the press.

Neruda's loyalty to communism caused him even greater trouble in South America. In 1957, Neruda was invited to attend the Congress for Peace in Ceylon. Because he had lived there in his youth and wanted to revisit some of the places he remembered, he accepted gladly. Unfortunately, he went by way of Buenos Aires, Argentina. He was then suffering from a return of the phlebitis that had been operated on just after the Spanish civil war and was in bed when the Argentine secret police suddenly broke into the house in which he was staying and arrested him. They carried him bodily out of the house and placed him in an ambulance that then took him to jail. In jail, Neruda was welcomed by his fellow prisoners, who seemed to have read his poetry. The Chilean consul as well as several Argentine writers complained strongly to the government, and Neruda was released the next day. No reason was given for his arrest, but it was obvious that he was not to be trusted in a "democratic" society.

Neruda made his first trip to the United States in 1966 when he was invited to an international congress of the P.E.N. organization that was held in New York City. The U.S. State Department refused to grant him entry at first but gave in after a storm of protest from the American members of P.E.N., led by playwright Arthur Miller and poet Marianne Moore. Neruda was made guest of honor for the occasion and, as he put it, "As always, I did what I had to do"[4]—read his poems. At the first public reading, the crowd was so great that a closed circuit television system had to be set up so that people outside could see and hear him. From New York he went to Washington, D.C., and then to Berkeley, California, where in addition to his readings he made tapes for the Library of Congress. He was greeted so warmly everywhere he went that he concluded that the American people shared his views on the world struggle. He did not pull any punches and openly criticized U.S. policy and condemned the war in Vietnam as one more example of United States imperialism.[5] The great majority of his audiences, however, were most likely applauding his poetry and his courage in defying unjust authority in his native land, not his political views.

When Neruda returned to Chile, he was shocked to receive a letter from a group of writers in Communist Cuba accusing him of treason in visiting the United States. The letter upset him considerably, and he made a strong reply to the writers, charging that "with arrogance, insolence, and flattering words they hoped to reform my poetry as well as my social revolutionary work." He scorned them as "newly come into the revolutionary camp, and many of them justly or unjustly in the pay of the new Cuban state."[6] This was the first time that Neruda had anything negative to say about his fellow Communists. In 1969, the Soviet Union crushed Czechoslovakia's attempt to achieve independence from the superpower that had controlled its government since the end of World War II. This also disturbed Neruda and caused him for the first time to doubt the Soviet Union's policies.

Neruda had thought that he was through with politics after his experience as a senator, but his popularity among the people had marked him as a likely candidate for any office. The Communist party of Chile was not strong enough to win an election, but it wanted to make a large enough showing to have some influence in a new government. The party leaders visited Neruda in Isla Negra to ask him to be their party's candidate for president. Neruda agreed, with the understanding that when a candidate appeared who had a better chance of winning for the Popular Unity party, of which the Communists were a part, he would withdraw and support that candidate. If such a candidate did not appear, then Neruda would campaign to the finish.

Neruda began campaigning immediately, and easily became the most popular candidate in the race, at least when it came to public appearances. Visiting factories and mines and making speeches before huge crowds brought Neruda face-to-face with the people he had been championing for years but had never actually known. Now he began to feel close to the populace and to wonder if it were possible that he could become president, and what he would do if he did. His problem was solved when Salvador Allende, a member of the Socialist party, emerged as the candidate who was most agreeable to all the different members of the Popular Unity party.

Neruda withdrew from the race for the presidency and threw his wholehearted support behind Allende. He knew the candidate well and had accompanied him on his previous campaigns for president. Now Neruda followed Allende everywhere, reading his own poetry and making speeches in favor of the Popular Unity party. Allende was a tireless campaigner and traveled the length of Chile to take his message to the people. He had run for president three times and was determined to win this time. His energy and determination paid off, for he received more votes than any of the other numerous candidates. He did not win a majority of the vote, however, which meant that the congress would have to choose the president. Normally, this would just be a matter of following the results of the election. The man who got the most votes would automatically be appointed by the congress. Unfortunately, other forces were at work in this election.

The president of the United States at that time was Richard M. Nixon, who had always had strong ties with conservative businessmen and megacorporations. He felt that Allende, with his moderate Socialist program, would be harmful to United States business interests in Chile, especially after Allende nationalized the American-owned copper mines. He and his secretary of state, Henry Kissinger, ended United States financial aid to Chile and blocked loans from nongovernment sources. It was widely reported in the international press that

In 1970, Neruda ran for the presidency of Chile and for the first time was able to take his message to the people.

the Nixon administration secretly worked to undermine Allende's government by financing opposition political groups in Chile and encouraging a military takeover by the Chilean army.[7] Neruda took this as further evidence of bad faith on the part of the United States in all its dealings with South America.

The new Allende government rewarded Neruda for his support by appointing him Chile's ambassador to France, a very important diplomatic post. Neruda accepted without really thinking about what it would cost him in time and effort. The position would have been difficult even for a younger man to fill, and Neruda was now sixty-six years old and in poor health. For years he had suffered from phlebitis, and now he was diagnosed as having prostate cancer. He looked forward to the Paris assignment, however, saying, "I was pleased at the idea of representing a victorious popular government, after so many years of mediocre and lying ones."[8] Although he was popular with everyone as a poet, there were still many people who were suspicious of his politics, which were much too far to the left to please some people in the Chilean government. His appointment as ambassador to France barely passed in the Senate. He won approval by only three votes.

Neruda was not in Paris long before talk began again about his receiving the Nobel Prize. "Every writer on this planet earth would really like to get the Nobel Prize sometime, whether he admits it or not,"[9] he later wrote. But he had been mentioned as a probable winner so often that he did not give it much thought. He was very careful, however, not to try to influence anyone on his behalf. His fellow Chilean and early teacher, Gabriela Mistral, had actively campaigned for the prize, which she was awarded in 1945, and had been criticized for her efforts. Nevertheless, on October 21, 1971, Neruda received a request from the

Swedish ambassador for an interview, and it was then revealed that he had been awarded the Nobel Prize for Literature. The official report read that the Swedish Academy had awarded the prize for a lifetime's work that had produced "poetry which like a force of nature gives new life to the destiny and dreams of an entire continent."[10]

Neruda underwent two operations while he was in Europe, and his health was obviously failing. After receiving his Nobel Prize in Stockholm, Sweden, he accepted an invitation from P.E.N. to appear in New York. In his speech there, Neruda attacked the economic blockade that the Nixon administration had imposed on Chile. Allende had fulfilled his promise to nationalize the great copper and nitrate industries by taking them out of the hands of foreigners and putting them into the hands of Chileans. The American corporations believed that they had not been offered enough in compensation for the industries they had created and financed, and they had brought pressure on President Nixon to punish Chile. The United States cut off all trade with Chile. Neruda was furious, and responded with his *Incitación al Nixonicidio y alabanza de la revolución chilena* (A call for the death of Nixon and praise for the Chilean Revolution). This was surely one of the harshest judgments ever delivered by a world-famous literary figure against a head of state.

Pablo Neruda and his wife, Matilde, met with Gunnar Haggloff (left), the Swedish ambassador, after being awarded the Nobel Prize for Literature in 1971.

Neruda decided to resign his post as ambassador to France and return to Chile. His declining health may have had much to do with this decision, but he also wanted to see many of his old friends who had made it clear that they wanted to celebrate his Nobel Prize with him in person. Shortly after arriving in Chile, he read his poems before a crowd in the National Stadium of Santiago and then retired to his home in Isla Negra. He was pleased with the warm welcome he received but disturbed by some of the things he now saw in Chile. Anticommunist and anti-Soviet posters had appeared in the major cities. The economic blockade by the United States was creating hardship for the middle class. The wealthy classes were recovering from their shock from Allende's victory and were slowly regaining their power by backing right-wing organizations and candidates. The general public was not at all pleased with the way Allende had imposed his socialist ideas on the nation. He had never been a majority candidate, and when things began to go wrong, it was easy for his lukewarm followers to turn against him.

In Isla Negra, Neruda could be close to the sea and the forests that he loved. He was visited often by President Allende, who was concerned over the declining health of his old friend. During Allende's last visit, in January 1973, Neruda read to him his poem calling for the death of Nixon. Allende thought that the poem was "gripping" but added: "Do you think, Pablo, that after publishing this book, you can go on being ambassador?" "Exactly," said Neruda, who was possibly the most undiplomatic diplomat who ever lived. "I'm asking that you relieve me of my office. I want and need to be in Chile."[11]

Neruda had been troubled and saddened by what he had seen of Chile's political situation, but he had not known just how serious it was. On September 11, 1973, Chilean military officers took over the government in a coup. Allende locked himself, his staff, and two of his granddaughters into La Moneda, the presidential palace. Soldiers under the command of General Augusto Pinochet quickly surrounded the palace and prepared for an all-out assault on the president, who was facing them alone. He had put on a steel helmet and had taken up a machine gun. He made a last-minute broadcast to the nation, vowing that he would never surrender. Neruda heard this broadcast in Isla Negra and was stunned. It was to be the last time he would hear the voice of his friend.

Allende, speaking over the telephone line to the guardhouse at the palace, addressed Pinochet directly, calling him a traitor but expecting him to let the women and children in the palace come out. The general hesitated but did decide to let the women and children pass through the ranks of soldiers surrounding the building. He then ordered an attack on the palace, beginning with an aerial bombardment. Allende died

Salvador Allende, Neruda's good friend, was president of Chile from 1970 until his death in 1973.

in the attack, but it is not known precisely how his end came about. Pinochet's forces say that they found Allende dead by his own hand. Neruda and many others denied this, claiming that he had been brutally assassinated by the soldiers. Shortly afterward, Neruda, imagining the scene, wrote that when the tanks of the assault force broke into the palace, Allende "was waiting for them in his office, with no other company but his great heart, surrounded by smoke and flame."[12]

General Pinochet and his fellow officers moved quickly to turn Chile into a military dictatorship. The government was suspended and Allende supporters were arrested. When resistance fighters arose in working-class neighborhoods, they were promptly put down by the army's tanks and planes. All the news media were taken over by the military and strictly censored. Chile became a closed camp, ruled by a military junta (council) that allowed no freedom of speech or action.[13] Most of the nations of the world were quick to condemn the junta. Most of them refused to recognize it and broke off diplomatic relations with Chile. The United States recognized the new government of Chile, making no secret of its approval of the overthrow of Allende's government. Aid and loans from the United States to the new regime increased spectacularly.[14]

Neruda was high on the list of the new government's enemies, and he received a visit from its representatives at once. Heavily armed soldiers broke into Neruda's home in Isla Negra and searched the house. What they were searching for was never made clear. Neruda was helpless. He could barely get out of bed and had witnessed most of the horrible news from the capital on television. When the soldiers left, his wife, Matilde, called for an ambulance to take Neruda to a hospital in Santiago. On the way, they were stopped repeatedly by soldiers, who searched the ambulance for subversive material. Neruda bore it all quietly but there were tears in his eyes.[15] He could do nothing to help his friends, who were being rounded up and confined in Santiago's National Stadium, the scene of many of Neruda's triumphs. The popular singer and guitarist Victor Jara, who had set some of Neruda's verses to music, was executed. Many of Neruda's friends simply disappeared, with no official explanation.

Neruda's houses were broken into and looted. His precious collections of artifacts and his valuable books were burned while he lay helpless in his hospital bed. Neruda was barely conscious, but he did manage to dictate the last pages of his memoirs, which he ended with a tribute to Allende and a condemnation of Chile's treacherous soldiers. The president of Mexico sent a special plane to have Neruda evacuated from Chile, but Neruda declined. He seemed more worried about having his memoirs preserved, and he lived to learn that the last pages were taken out of Chile in a diplomatic pouch. On the night before his death, he lay in his bed in the hospital listening to the helicopters flying back and forth over the city. In his delirium, he kept repeating, "They're shooting them, they're killing them."[16] He died of a heart attack on September 23, 1973, at the age of sixty-nine.

Neruda's body was taken to his ruined house in Santiago, where it was put on view for friends and neighbors. The house and the streets outside were crowded with mourners. Dignitaries and associates arrived quietly, trying not to be observed. Everyone there knew they were under suspicion of being a friend of an enemy of the new government, but they came anyway. The next day, as Neruda's coffin was being carried to the cemetery, the crowd began a roll call of Chilean heroes who had died for their country. After each name, the crowd answered, "Present."

"Comrade Salvador Allende," the crowd shouted.

"Present," came the reply.

"Comrade Pablo Neruda."

"PRESENT!" the crowd roared.[17]

For years Neruda's works were officially banned in Chile, which was a futile gesture by the new government because his poems were known everywhere throughout the world. His memoirs were published shortly after his death and were immediately translated into all the major languages. Volumes of his unpublished poetry continued to be published and were added to the astonishing complete works.

General Pinochet remained in power until 1986, when through a provision of his own constitution, he reluctantly agreed to a presidential election, which he expected to win. He was defeated at the polls, however, but still remains a force in the new government. Chile has since rebounded both economically and politically. It is on friendly terms with all the other nations of South America and has renewed diplomatic relations with the rest of the world. Chile's prolonged journey back to democracy has been completed, and the works of Pablo Neruda are now considered one of its national treasures.

CHAPTER NINE

FINAL

 Today, Pablo Neruda is recognized as Chile's greatest poet and is read freely and widely in his own country. His home in Santiago, La Chascona, has been restored and is now a museum as well as the headquarters of the Pablo Neruda Foundation. The foundation manages Neruda's huge literary estate and regularly handles requests from all over the world for permissions and requests for the use of some aspect of his life and works. His complete poetical works make up three volumes totaling 3,552 pages.

Neruda did not die a happy man. His hopes and ambitions for Chile were crushed with the overthrow of the Allende government. With the collapse of Soviet communism in Europe, popular fronts such as Chile's have been seriously weakened or have ceased to exist. Neruda's political views as well as his passionate writings and poems in defense of communism have become outdated and are of little interest except to scholars and students of Neruda's life. His great lyric and epic writings, however, are another matter. They continue to inspire, move, inform, and entertain general readers everywhere, and his work is beginning to be ranked with that of the greatest literary figures of the twentieth century.

In 1995, Neruda achieved even more fame and gained more readers through the unlikely medium of the motion picture. A modest Italian film by the title of *Il postino* (The postman) was released with little fanfare but gained international renown. It tells the story of a lonely young man who lives on a remote island in the Mediterranean. He seems destined for a life of monotony until a celebrity comes to live there. It is Pablo Neruda, accompanied by a woman whom he addresses only as "Amor." Since hardly anyone on the island is able to read, they have had little need for a postman. With Neruda's arrival, however, there is suddenly a flood of mail addressed to him, and the young man is hired to deliver it. The postman soon notices that most of Neruda's mail is from women, and he decides that he might like to become a poet himself. The young

President Richard M. Nixon and his secretary of state, Henry Kissinger, supported the overthrow of Salvador Allende's government.

man and the poet soon grew to know and respect each other, and the poet teaches the postman of the beauty of his island and his life. The postman, in turn, touches the poet with his simplicity and truthfulness. It is a simple and charming tale, and communicates a love of poetry and beauty from both sides of the social and intellectual barriers between the two characters.

Shortly after the film was released to theaters in the United States, a CD recording was made of the sound track of the movie. This is nothing unusual for a popular movie, but in this case it was very different. Twelve Hollywood and pop music stars, ranging from Andy García to Madonna, and from Julia Roberts to Sting, are heard reading a selection of Neruda's poems. Thus a whole new generation, whose artistic experiences have been dominated by motion pictures and popular music, has been given the opportunity to listen to and to read the poetry of Pablo Neruda.

Neruda was a passionate man who led a life full of romance and controversy and was at the center of some of the twentieth century's great events. He will probably be portrayed often in future dramatizations, either in movies or on television, or on the stage. Like most great artists, he had his weaknesses, but these added an extra dimension to his achievements. But after all his politics and his personal loves and hates are forgotten, he will remain a poet who wrote about the things of this world that truly matter. To him, these

General Augusto Pinochet, who overthrew the government of Allende in 1973, remained Chile's president until 1986.

were love, death, the sea, the forests, and the teeming life of the earth.

He began as a writer of love poems and then turned his attention inward to become an extremely personal poet, expressing his inner state of mind in sometimes difficult and obscure language. After his experiences in Spain during its civil war, he became a public and political poet, speaking out against the injustices of his time. In the happy days of his last marriage and domestic peace, he turned to autobiography in *Memorial de Isla Negra* and to the celebration of ordinary, everyday things in *Odas elementales* (Elemental odes). His *Cien sonetos de amor* (One hundred love sonnets) continued his tribute to earthly love and human devotion. Through it all, he remained a Chilean poet who never ceased to describe, identify with, and wonder at his native land.

His last poem was called *"Final"* (The end) and was written just before his death. It was dedicated to his wife Matilde, but it could be meant for anyone in his huge and devoted audience:

Fue tan bello vivir
cuando vivías.[1]

[It was so good to live
when you lived.]

CHRONOLOGY

1904—Born Neftalí Ricardo Reyes Basoalto on July 12 in Parral, Chile. His mother dies one month later.

1906—His father remarries and moves his family to Temuco.

1910—Neftalí enters Temuco's school for boys.

1919—Thirteen of his poems appear in the Santiago magazine *Corre-Vuela*.

1920—He takes the name Pablo Neruda; wins first prize in Temuco's spring festival.

1921—He moves to Santiago to study French at the Teachers Institute.

1924—*Veinte poemas de amor y una canción desesperada* is published.

1927—He receives appointment as consul in Rangoon, Burma, and leaves for Far East via Spain and France.

1928—He is made consul in Colombo, Ceylon.

1930—He is made consul in Batavia, Java, and marries María Antonieta Hagenaar Vogelzanz.

1931—He is made consul in Singapore.

1932—He returns with his wife to Santiago.

1933—He is appointed consul in Argentina. Limited edition of *Residencia en la tierra* is published in Buenos Aires. He meets Federico García Lorca.

1934— He is appointed consul in Barcelona, Spain. His daughter, Malva Marina is born.

1935—He is appointed consul in Madrid.

1936— Spanish civil war begins; Federico García Lorca is killed by Nationalists; he is dismissed from his consular post.

1937—He separates from María Antonieta Hagenaar Vogelzanz and after their divorce marries Argentine painter Delia del Carril; organizes International Writers Congress in Madrid; *España en el corazón* published; returns to Chile.

1939— Appointed consul in charge of emigration of Spanish refugees; manages to get two thousand safely to Chile.

1940—He is appointed general consul in Mexico.

1943— Resigns his post in Mexico and returns to Chile, on the way stopping in Peru to visit Machu Picchu.

1945— He is elected to the Chilean Senate and joins the Communist party.

1947— Defies Chilean president González Videla and denounces him in an open letter.

1948—He is ordered arrested as a Communist agitator and goes into hiding.

1949—Flees across border to Argentina and moves to Europe; travels widely and visits Soviet Union.

1950—*Canto general* is published in Mexico.

1952—New government in Chile revokes the order for his arrest, and he returns to Santiago.

1954— He divorces Delia del Carril and moves into his new house in Santiago with Matilde Urrutia.

1957—He is arrested in Buenos Aires while on his way to the Far East but is released after the Chilean consul and Argentine writers complain.

1966—Visits the United States for the first time as guest of honor of the P.E.N. organization in New York.

1970—He runs for president of Chile but steps aside when Salvador Allende enters the race. Appointed ambassador to France after Allende's victory.

1971—He is awarded the Nobel Prize for Literature.

1972—He returns to Chile and retires to Isla Negra.

1973—Allende's government is overthrown, and he dies during attack on the presidential palace on September 11. Pinochet named dictator. Neruda dies in a hospital in Santiago on September 23.

CHAPTER NOTES

CHAPTER 1. THE FUGITIVE

1. Pablo Neruda, *Memoirs* (New York: Farrar, Straus and Giroux, 1976, 1977), p. 173.

2. Joseph Roman, *Pablo Neruda* (New York: Chelsea House, 1992), p. 73.

3. Neruda, p. 177.

4. Marjorie Agostin, *Pablo Neruda* (Boston: Twayne, 1986), p. 8. Quoted from Neruda's Nobel Prize Lecture, 1971.

5. Neruda, p. 184.

CHAPTER 2. THE FOREST AND THE SEA

1. Pablo Neruda, *Memoirs* (New York: Farrar, Straus and Giroux, 1976, 1977), p. 10.

2. From *"La poesía," Memorial de Isla Negra.* All quotations are from Pablo Neruda, *Obras Completas* (Buenos Aires: Editorial Losada, S.A., 1964). Reprinted by permission of the Pablo Neruda Foundation.

3. Joseph Roman, *Pablo Neruda* (New York: Chelsea House, 1992), p. 27.

4. Neruda, p. 21.

5. Volodia Teitelboim, *Neruda: An Intimate Biography* (Austin: University of Texas Press, 1991), p. 30.

6. Ibid.

7. Neruda, p. 21.

8. Ibid., p. 4.

9. Teitelboim, p. 27.

10. Neruda, p. 16.

11. Roman, p. 30.

12. Neruda, p. 21.

13. Ibid., p. 29.

14. From *"Il tren nocturno," Memorial de Isla Negra.*

CHAPTER 3. FROM POET TO DIPLOMAT

1. Pablo Neruda, *Memoirs* (New York: Farrar, Straus and Giroux, 1976, 1977), p. 30.

2. Ibid.

3. Ibid., p. 52

4. Harold Bloom., ed., *Pablo Neruda* (New York: Chelsea House, 1989), p. 84.

5. Rex A. Hudson, ed., *Chile: A Country Study* (Washington, D.C.: Federal Research Division, Library of Congress, 1994), p. 31.

6. Joseph Roman, *Pablo Neruda* (New York: Chelsea House, 1992), p. 38.

7. Neruda, p. 65.

8. Ibid., pp. 65–66.

CHAPTER 4. TO THE FAR EAST AND BACK

1. Pablo Neruda, *Memoirs* (New York: Farrar, Straus and Giroux, 1976, 1977), pp. 46–48.

2. Ibid., p. 75.

3. Ibid., p. 87.

4. Joseph Roman, *Pablo Neruda* (New York: Chelsea House, 1992), p. 47.

5. Neruda, p. 86.

6. From *"Tango del viudo," Residencia en la tierra.* All quotations are from Pablo Neruda, *Obras Completas* (Buenos Aires: Editorial Losada, S.A., 1964). Reprinted by permission of the Pablo Neruda Foundation.

7. Neruda, p. 91.

8. Ibid., p. 96.

9. Ibid., p. 107.

10. Ibid., p. 109.

CHAPTER 5. SPAIN IN THE HEART

1. Volodia Teitelboim, *Neruda: An Intimate Biography* (Austin: University of Texas Press, 1991), p. 154.

2. Pablo Neruda, *Memoirs* (New York: Farrar, Straus and Giroux, 1976, 1977), p. 116.

3. Teitelboim, p. 172.

4. Ibid., pp. 173–175.

5. Neruda, p. 122.

6. Ibid., p. 132.

7. From *"El padre," Memorial de Isla Negra*. All quotations are from Pablo Neruda, *Obras Completas* (Buenos Aires: Editorial Losada, S.A., 1964). Reprinted by permission of the Pablo Neruda Foundation.

8. Neruda, p. 140.

9. Teitelboim, p. 447.

10. Neruda, p. 140.

11. Ibid.

12. Ibid.

13. Ibid., p. 146.

CHAPTER 6. THE HEIGHTS OF MACHU PICCHU

1. Volodia Teitelboim, *Neruda: An Intimate Biography* (Austin: University of Texas Press, 1991), p. 245.

2. Ibid., p. 247.

3. Pablo Neruda, *Memoirs* (New York: Farrar, Straus and Giroux, 1976, 1977), p. 164.

4. From *"Alturas de Macchu Picchu," Canto general*. All quotations are from Pablo Neruda, *Obras Completas* (Buenos Aires: Editorial Losada, S.A., 1964). Reprinted by permission of the Pablo Neruda Foundation.

5. Neruda, p. 166.

6. Ibid., p. 171.

CHAPTER 7. EXILE AND RETURN

1. Volodia Teitelboim, *Neruda: An Intimate Biography* (Austin: University of Texas Press, 1991), p. 294.

2. Joseph Roman, *Pablo Neruda* (New York: Chelsea House, 1992), p. 75.

3. Pablo Neruda, *Memoirs* (New York: Farrar, Straus and Giroux, 1976, 1977), p. 190.

4. Teitelboim, p. 336.

5. Rex A. Hudson, ed., *Chile: A Country Study* (Washington, D.C.: Federal Research Division, Library of Congress, 1994), p. 41.

CHAPTER 8. HONORS, HOPE, AND DESPAIR

1. Pablo Neruda, *Memoirs* (New York: Farrar, Straus and Giroux, 1976, 1977), p. 216.
2. Ibid., p. 161.
3. Volodia Teitelboim, *Neruda: An Intimate Biography* (Austin: University of Texas Press, 1991), pp. 412–413.
4. Neruda, p. 325.
5. Ibid.
6. Ibid., p. 326.
7. Rex A. Hudson, ed., *Chile: A Country Study* (Washington, D.C.: Federal Research Division, Library of Congress, 1994), pp. 48–49.
8. Joseph Roman, *Pablo Neruda* (New York: Chelsea House, 1992), p. 92.
9. Neruda, p. 302.
10. Teitelboim, p. 439.
11. Ibid., p. 454.
12. Neruda, p. 350.
13. Hudson, p. 52.
14. Ibid., p. 53.
15. Teitelboim, p. 468.
16. Ibid., p. 469.
17. Ibid., pp. 476–477.

CHAPTER 9. *FINAL*

1. From *"Final,"* *La mar y las campanas.* All quotations are from Pablo Neruda, *Obras Completas* (Buenos Aires: Editorial Losada, S.A., 1964). Reprinted by permission of the Pablo Neruda Foundation.

x

GLOSSARY

anarchist—A person opposed to all forms of government.

aristocrat—A person who holds rank or privileges above the ordinary, usually by inheritance.

communism—A form of government in which all property is held in common, with actual ownership given to the state.

conservative—A person who favors keeping the existing conditions and government; traditional in style or manner.

coup—The sudden overthrow of a government by force.

epic poetry—Poetry that celebrates the history of a people or nation in a grand or elevated style.

fascism—A system of government led by a dictator and claiming absolute control over the people of a country.

Inca—A dominant people of South America who established an empire in Peru prior to the Spanish conquest.

junta—A group of people that runs a country, usually after a coup.

leftist—A person who favors reform or revolutionary change in government, usually to bring about improved social conditions.

liberal—A person who favors progress or reform in government.

lyric poetry—Poetry written in the form of song and expressing the poet's feelings in personal language.

monarchy—A government presided over by a king or a queen.

reformist—A person who favors a gradual change in government to make it more efficient or to better represent the people.

republic—A government conducted by representatives elected by the people of a country.

rightist—A person who holds traditional or conservative political views.

socialist—A person who believes that ownership of all land, industry, and capital should be held by the people as a whole.

united front—Different political parties or groups that come together to oppose a common danger or enemy.

FURTHER READING

Agostin, Marjorie. *Pablo Neruda*. Boston: Twayne, 1986.

Bloom, Harold, ed. *Pablo Neruda*. New York: Chelsea House, 1989.

Costa, René de. *The Poetry of Pablo Neruda*. Cambridge: Harvard University Press, 1979.

Durán, Manuel, and Margery Safir. *Earth Tones: The Poetry of Pablo Neruda*. Bloomington: Indiana University Press, 1981.

Hudson, Rex A., ed. *Chile: A Country Study*. Washington, D.C.: Federal Research Division, Library of Congress, 1994.

Pablo Neruda. *Five Decades: Poems, 1925–1970*. Translated by Ben Bellitt. New York: Grove Press, 1974.

———. *The Heights of Macchu Picchu*. Translated by Nathaniel Tarn. New York: Farrar, Straus and Giroux, 1966.

———. *Isla Negra: A Notebook*. Translated by Alastair Reid. New York: Farrar, Straus and Giroux, 1981.

———. *Memoirs*. Translated by Hardie St. Martin. New York: Farrar, Straus and Giroux, 1977.

———. *Residence on Earth*. Translated by Donald D. Walsh. New York: New Directions, 1973.

————. *Twenty Love Poems and a Song of Despair*. New York: Norton, 1990.

Roman, Joseph. *Pablo Neruda*. New York: Chelsea House, 1992.

Santi, Enrico M. *Pablo Neruda: The Politics of Prophecy*. Ithaca: Cornell University Press, 1982.

Teitelboim, Volodia. *Neruda: An Intimate Biography*. Translated by Beverly J. DeLong-Tonelli. Austin: University of Texas Press, 1991.

INDEX